MYSTIC

CATS

A CELEBRATION OF
CAT MAGIC & FELINE CHARM

RONI JAY

ILLUSTRATED BY
LORRAINE HARRISON

HarperSanFrancisco
A Division of HarperCollins*Publishers*

Mystic Cats: *A Celebration of Cat Magic and Feline Charm*

Copyright © 1995 *Godsfield Press Ltd*

Text © 1995 *Roni Jay*
Illustrations © 1995 *Lorraine Harrison*
Originally published by Godsfield Press Ltd 1995
Designed by *The Bridgewater Book Company Ltd*

 A GODSFIELD PRESS BOOK

1

First Edition

Library of Congress Cataloging-in-Publication Data

Jay, Roni.
    Mystic cats: a celebration of cat magic and feline charm / Roni Jay. -- 1st ed.
        p. cm.
    ISBN 0-06-251210-2 (cloth : acid-free paper)
    1. Cats -- Folklore.   I. Title.
GR725.J39 1995
398' .369974428 -- dc20   94-34317
                                                               CIP

95 96 97 98 99 GDP 10 9 8 7 6 5 4 3 2 1

CONTENTS

INTRODUCTION

*C*ats were first
domesticated in Egypt
about 3,500 years ago.
*Since then they have been both deified and vilified around the
world. The domestic cat increased its territory from North Africa
to Europe and Asia, and subsequently the Americas and the
Pacific - and many of the Egyptians' beliefs about cats travelled
with them. Consequently, cats have been incorporated into many
of the most complex mystic, mythical, religious and magical beliefs
of the last few thousand years. Mystic Cats explores many of these
fascinating beliefs, uncovering many unusual reasons for them.*

*How did this extraordinary relationship with cats build up?
Cats initially became domesticated because of the ready supply of
food. The arrangement was mutual - we wanted the rats and mice
killed and the cats were willing executioners. Even the Egyptians
were not always above getting value from their cats - they used
them to guard their grain stores. But why have we always been
prone to treat cats with such respect - at times even awe?
There do seem to be other, less obvious links between
cats and humans that may explain why the ancient
Egyptians took so naturally to treating cats as gods.*

For one thing cats are closer to their wild roots than most domestic animals. The number of feral cats in modern cities demonstrates that cats can still revert quickly to their wild state and survive adequately. This feeling that cats don't really need us may well explain why people consider it such an honour when cats treat them with affection.

Cats also have a therapeutic effect on people, although no one is quite certain why. Research has clearly shown that stroking a cat reduces people's blood pressure and eases stress. The Egyptians may not have had the scientific data, but they presumably recognized the psychological benefit. It seems that touching is very important, both to us and to cats, and our relationships with them tend to be very tactile. Psychologically, too, cats can form relationships with humans in a way that is reminiscent of our own friendships with each other.

Mystic Cats takes a closer look at some of the stranger ways that our relationship with cats has manifested itself in the past. Read on . . .

CATS IN CREATION

According to Hebrew folk-lore, there were no cats on earth before the great flood. However, once all the other animals were aboard the Ark, Noah became concerned that the lion would threaten the other creatures. He prayed for help, and God responded by sending the lion into a deep sleep. But this created a new problem: the number of rats began to increase, quickly threatening to eat the supplies.

Again Noah asked God for help, and He told Noah to hit the lion across the nose. This made the lion sneeze, and out of its nostrils came the first two cats – the perfect solution to the rat problem.

Not surprisingly, many stories about the creation of cats associate them with lions. The cat's other common association in creation myths is with the moon. According to one tale, the cat was the result of a competition between the sun and the moon to create the best animal. First, the sun impressed all the gods by creating the lion. Then the moon, jealous of the gods' admiration for the sun, created a cat. But the gods laughed at what they considered a poor imitation of a lion. The sun showed his contempt by creating a mouse, and the moon, still trying to impress, created a monkey – which the gods found even funnier. So the moon, in fury, caused her animals and the sun's to hate each other, which is why monkeys and lions dislike each other – and so do cats and mice.

DEALINGS WITH THE DEVIL

Christianity, of course, replaced the duality of sun and moon with good and bad. The dog was the good creation of God, while the cat was the bad creation of the Devil. There was a medieval belief that Satan invented the cat by mistake. He was trying to create a man, but produced a hairless cat instead. St. Peter felt sorry for the cat, however, and gave it a fur coat.

The Mongolian shamans believed that God made the first man and woman out of clay covered with fur. In order to bring them to life, He had to fetch water from the eternal spring, so He posted the cat and the dog to guard the clay man and woman while He was gone. The Devil, however, distracted them with offerings of meat and milk and then urinated on them. God was so angry that He made the cat lick off all the soiled fur – except the hair on the man and woman's heads, which were clean. The cat couldn't quite reach all the fur, so it had to leave a little on the groin and under armpits. God put the fur on the dog and then brought the man and woman to life with the sacred water. But because they had been defiled, He couldn't give humans immortality.

THE REAL CAT

What is it about cats that has given rise to so many mystic and magical beliefs about them? Cats have numerous qualities that people seem to have found difficult to explain and, therefore, have attributed to unusual or even divine powers.

One of the cat's most extraordinary abilities is that it always falls on its feet – recent research found that 90 percent of cats that fall from skyscrapers in New York survive. There is a legend that on one occasion when Mohammed needed to go out, he found his pet cat Muezza asleep on his coat. Rather than disturb her, he cut the sleeve off so she could continue her catnap. When he came home, Muezza was so grateful that she stood up and bowed to him (if you've ever seen a cat stretch itself on waking up, you can imagine how this looked). Mohammed was deeply touched, and as a reward he granted all cats the ability to land on their feet.

Cats have been a symbol of fertility in cultures around the world. This view of them is supported by their behavior; a female cat can produce two or even three litters of kittens a year for most of her life. All mammals, of course, need to be sexually active to perpetuate the species, but cats appear to be more enthusiastic and less discreet about it than most.

Cats are particularly independent for domestic animals; almost to the point of aloofness. They are descended from highly territorial ancestors and, consequently, are often more attached to places than the people they live with; cats will sometimes give up their human companions far more readily than their territory. This self-contained independence can give them an air of self-importance that tends to generate respect – even admiration. ♪

THE CAT'S SENSES

Cats like to go out at night, and they have exceptional eyesight that allows them to see far better than we do in dim light. This fondness for night-time wandering has given cats an air of mystery and an association with the subconscious, or darker side, of nature. Cats also have a highly developed sense of hearing that can detect sounds far outside the human range. At times, this has led people to believe that cats have supernatural powers, or at least a "sixth sense." For example, cats seem to be able to sense thunderstorms before we can. In fact, the cats probably hear the first storm vibrations at a frequency outside our hearing range. Their sensitive hearing also gives cats an uncanny ability to distinguish sounds such as a particular person's footsteps, a special car or a can opener being taken out of a drawer.

FELINE INTELLIGENCE

There's no doubt that cats are intelligent animals. Not only can they learn by copying, they can also solve problems. And once cats have learned the solutions, they can adapt and apply them to other similar problems.

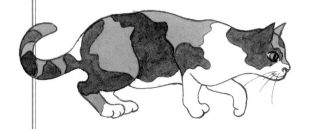

In spite of this intelligence, cats have a singular reluctance to learn unless there's something in it for them. Unlike dogs, for example, cats are notoriously difficult to train and can be motivated only by reward, not punishment. Even that is hard, since food is the only incentive that tends to work, and cats would often rather hunt than eat the food we provide. Chaucer recognized this back in the 14th century, when he wrote:

> *Let take a cat and foster him well with milk*
> *and tender flesh, and make his couch of silk,*
> *And let him see a mouse go by the wall;*
> *Anon he waveth milk, and flesh, and all,*
> *And every dainty that is in the house,*
> *Such appetite hath he to eat a mouse.*

This untrainable intelligence, coupled with their highly developed skill and enthusiasm as hunters, has earned cats a reputation for stealth and even wiliness. It also makes them worthy to be treated as gods – or agents of the Devil, depending on the part of the world and the period of history.

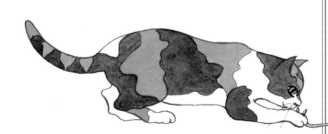

CATS' EYES

The Romans believed that cats' eyes – or even their whole bodies – changed in accordance with the phases of the moon. Plutarch wrote that although it might seem fanciful, nevertheless, "it can be depended upon that the pupils of her eyes appear to fill up and grow large upon the full moon and to decrease again and reduce their brightness as it wanes."

In fact, cats' eyes have a mirrored layer of cells behind the retina that increases their ability to see in low light. It is this layer that reflects the light and makes cats' eyes seem to glow. The pupils of their eyes also dilate in dim light and contract in bright light over a wide size range, which has led to the belief that they wax and wane according to the phases of the moon. It was even thought in some places, including parts of eastern England, that cats' eyes changed size to mark the ebb and flow of the tide.

A French missionary in China in the last century once asked some village children what the time was. They promptly rounded up a local cat, pried open its eyes and informed him that it was still morning. The children claimed that cats' pupils grow thinner and thinner until noon, when they gradually start to dilate again. Of course, there is a grain of truth in this, since cats' eyes are at their thinnest when the light is brightest.

The Egyptians thought that cats held the sun's rays in their eyes at night. To the superstitious Christians of the Middle Ages, cats had demonic glittering eyes, and, according to one writer of the time, "in the night they can hardly be endured for their flaming aspect."

CAT'S-EYE STONES

In the Middle Ages, many animals had gemstones associated with them. There is a kind of stone, closely related to the tiger's-eye but a different color, called a cat's-eye. It is made of a fibrous quartz colored with olive green streaks of hornblende-asbestos. When cut, curved and polished, it looks something like an iridescent shining eye.

Many beliefs have been held about this stone. In medieval times it was worn as an amulet to ward off witchcraft – perhaps to turn the evil eye back on whoever was casting it. The Arabs, perhaps through a similar sympathetic magic, believed that a cat's-eye stone made them invisible in battle. And in some places, men who had to travel away from home for some time would make their wives drink milk that had a cat's-eye stone dipped in it. Interestingly, this wasn't intended to guarantee their wives' fidelity but only to ensure that any adultery would not lead to children. This practice clearly relates to the association between cats and fertility.

THE SYMBOLISM OF CATS

Cats have been a part of human society for 3,500 years, so it's hardly surprising that they have come to represent many things to many cultures. Much of the symbolism shows that the cat's basic nature has hardly changed in all that time. They have long been associated with certain ideals – such as liberty, for example – because of traits of character that can still be seen in 20th-century domestic cats.

THE UNCONSCIOUS

Cats were always linked with the unconscious rather than conscious, the moon rather than the sun, yin rather than yang. The Egyptians believed the cat-headed goddess Bastet was the moon, the left eye of the sky god Horus who guarded the world at night while his right eye, the sun, slept. The left eye, and left side of the body, is governed by the intuitive, creative right hemisphere of the brain.

FERTILITY

Cats have traditionally represented fertility. Beside the obvious fact that cats are prolific breeders, there is another particularly interesting reason for linking cats with fertility. The changing shapes of their eyes have been associated with the moon, and therefore with women, whose menstrual cycle was always considered to be linked to the lunar cycle.

Most fascinating of all, though, the Egyptian hieroglyph for birth, which was called "Ru," was apparently drawn from the shape of a cat's eye and represents an opening or doorway – either the birth canal or the gateway to the physical plane from the spiritual plane (which was governed by the moon). This clearly links cats with birth. Furthermore, it seems that the hieroglyph Ru was placed on top of the Tau cross, which signifies time in the physical plane, to create the ankh, which symbolizes life and immortality. The ancient ankh symbol was adapted to represent Venus, the archetypal woman, and is a symbol we still use today. In view of all this symbolism, the close ties between cats and fertility is hardly surprising.

LIBERTY

It was probably because of the cat's inherent independence, and its wild nature, that the cat was used as a symbol of liberty by the Romans and, later, in heraldry. It was at various times the emblem of the Vandals, the Suevi and the Dutch, among others. The Dutch had fought so long to achieve freedom and independence that they came to identify with the cat's love of freedom and adopted the cat as their symbol.

The goddess Artemis was the Greek equivalent of the Egyptian cat goddess Bastet. Artemis stood for freedom, wildness, nature and the hunting instinct – all good feline qualities. The Romans turned Artemis into their goddess of the hunt, Diana, who was often pictured with a cat at her feet representing liberty.

WATCHFULNESS

Bastet, in her role as the moon, spent every night gazing down impassively from the heavens – just as a cat will watch a mouse or a bird for hours on end, or sit looking out a window. Consequently, cats became associated with detached attentiveness.

STEALTH

Cats' skill as hunters, their curiosity and their inventiveness have earned them a reputation for stealth and mystery the world over. In Aesop's fables the cat is the trickster, and the enterprising Puss in Boots (himself an alchemical allegory) brings his master fame and fortune through his scheming. Perhaps one of the reasons that current stories about big cats on the loose catch the public imagination is that they fit so neatly into our conventional view of cats as stealthy and secretive.

ETERNITY

The circle has no beginning and no end; every point on the circle can be both a beginning and an end. For this reason the circle has long been considered a symbol of eternity. To Zen Buddhists the circle represents enlightenment. The Chinese yin yang symbol forms a circle, showing that when everything is in balance you have unity and perfection. Cats sometimes symbolize eternity because often when they sleep they curl themselves up nose to tail and create an unbroken circle. Interestingly, as far

as the balance of nature is concerned, the people of the Cotswolds in the English Midlands used to believe that you should keep both a black and a white cat for balance.

THE SYMBOLISM OF CAT AND MOUSE

Of course, the main reasons that cats are often depicted in the act of hunting mice is simply because that is what they do. But the image is sometimes used symbolically; the mouse represents the human soul, and the cat represents death, picking off some mice suddenly, and playing with others before finally killing them. In parts of Europe, mice were thought to be the souls of the dead, and people often put food out for them.

MODERN WESTERN SYMBOLISM

To see how cats are viewed in the modern Western world, you need only look at advertisements that feature cats. Cats are used to represent sensuality and luxury – a love of pleasure well suited to their character. Also according to the ads, we associate cats with women rather than men.

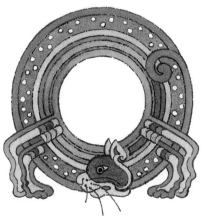

SACRED BREEDS

Probably the most famous sacred cats were those kept by the Egyptians. The modern Abyssinian breed, which comes from Ethiopia, may be a direct descendent of the ancient cats of Egypt. However, some people believe that the modern Abyssinian look was created by mating tabbies. Either way, Abyssinian cats certainly look more like the ancient sacred cats than any other breed does.

The claim that the Abyssinian was the first domestic cat is supported by the cat's unusual coat. It was sometimes known as the "hare-cat" because of its characteristic ticked fur – every hair has two or three dark-colored bands. This type of coat is also typical of the African wildcat, the species from which the domestic cat is thought to be descended.

THE TEMPLE CATS
Both Siamese and Birman cats were revered as the guardians of Buddhist temples. The people of Thailand believed that people's spirits transferred – or "transmigrated" – into cats when they died. This of course made cats sacred – they

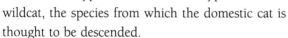

might not really be cats at all, but human souls in cats' bodies. Members of the royal family of Siam used to be buried with a live cat. The roof of the burial chamber contained small holes; if the cat escaped through one of them it was seen as evidence that the royal soul had passed into the cat.

The Burmese believed that transmigration was responsible for the appearance of the Birman cat. The story goes that before the birth of the Buddha, the temple of Lao Tsun, dedicated to the worship of the blue-eyed goddess Tsun Kyankse who oversaw the transmigration of departing souls, had a hundred white cats. One night, raiders attacked the temple and killed the high priest as he knelt at the altar. His yellow-eyed cat, Sinh, immediately leaped onto the priest's body, and his soul entered into the cat. The cat's fur became golden, and its eyes blue, like the goddess. But where it had touched the body of the priest, its feet remained pure white, as a symbol of the priest's purity. The high priest, in Sinh's body, inspired his priests to overcome the raiders. Sinh sat on the throne for seven days, refusing all food, and at the end of a week he died. His master's soul passed on to heaven. But from that time on, all the other cats of the temple became blue-eyed, with golden fur – and the distinctive white feet of the Birman cat.

THE SUN AND THE MOON

Cats are apparently able to see in the dark, which has given them a strong association with the light-giving sun and moon. Their reflective eyes, which supposedly store the sun's light and reflect it back at night, are also reputed to wax and wane with the phases of the moon.

The cat's links with both the sun and the moon can be traced back to the Egyptians. They, like many other cultures, associated lions with the sun because both are strong and powerful. The great Egyptian sun god, Ra, was often represented as a lion, as was his daughter Sekhmet, the merciless destroyer of his enemies.

It seems likely that one of the reasons that the Egyptians began to domesticate and worship cats is because they were seen as little lions. In 2000 B.C. the African wildcat would have looked even more like a lion than today's domestic cats do. As a result, cats came to represent the same things that lions did, and Ra often took the form of a cat. However, since cats were little lions, they were also identified with the moon – a little sun. The cat became the symbol of the moon goddess Bastet (who had originally been worshiped in the form of a lion).

Sekhmet and Bastet were sisters, collectively known as "the eyes of Horus." Horus was the great sky god. Sekhmet, the lion-headed goddess was his right eye – the sun – gazing down on the earth during the day, and Bastet was his left eye – the moon – which was visible by night. Bastet was also regarded sometimes as being the left eye of the moon goddess Isis.

CATS AND THE WEATHER

It's hard to say how much truth there is in the idea that cats can predict the weather. They are more sensitive than we are to changes in levels of static electricity, and perhaps barometric pressure, and they often seem to know when a storm is coming – cats have even been known to move their kittens away from the path of a tornado shortly before it strikes. However, most of the folklore about their weather forecasting skills seems to be based on less convincing factors.

There is a widespread belief that rain is on the way if a cat puts its paw behind its ear (which all cats do when they wash). The cat is sometimes described as "pulling down the rain" when it does this. A cat acting wildly with "the wind up its tail" is a sign of a storm, and the position a cat sits in, or the way it washes, can variously foretell rain, snow, frost, storm or other bad weather.

In Scotland and Eastern Europe it was thought that lightning bolts were sent by angels to rid cats of the evil spirits that possessed them. So the cats were always put outside during storms to prevent lightning from striking the house.

Many traditions hold that cats not only predict the weather but can actually influence it. This notion seems to stem from the supposed relationship between cats and witches, who were thought to have this power. Some of the folklore tells of cat bringing rain for the crops to grow, and this branch of belief may derive from the ancient cat goddesses who looked after the crops.

In Cambodia there was an old tradition of taking a cat from village to village in a cage to be sprinkled with water by the villagers. This was supposed to encourage the god Indra to send the rain. In many countries bathing a cat, or ducking it in water, was believed to cause rain.

CATS AT NIGHT

Every night Ra, the sun, goes to sleep and the land becomes dark, or so the ancient Egyptians believed. As Ra passes through the underworld on his barge, accompanied by spirits of the dead, the serpent Apep tries to stop him by drinking the water under the boat. But the Great Cat appears and cuts off Apep's head – cheered on by the spirits crying "miaow"– thereby enabling the sun to rise again over Egypt each morning.

VAMPIRE CATS

Japanese vampires often appear as cats and subsequently take on the form of their victims. In one typical story, the Prince of Hizen spends the evening with his favorite lady, O Toyo. When they separate at the end of the evening a gigantic black cat follows O Toyo and strangles her. The cat then assumes her shape and continues to meet the prince every evening. At each meeting it bewitches the prince and then sucks his blood. He becomes gradually weaker until finally a loyal soldier realizes that the prince has been charmed and kills the vampire.

This Japanese view of vampires may be connected with the Chinese belief that if a corpse is laid on a bed that has a dog under it and a cat on the roof above it, the dead person will rise for a short time and perform evil deeds. And in many parts of Europe there is a belief that if a cat walks over a corpse it will become a vampire – which is why it's customary to shut cats out of rooms that have corpses in them.

One well-documented case of vampirism from 15th-century Eastern Europe tells of strange hauntings, and even murder, by the spirit of a man whose face had been violently scratched by a black cat at the moment of his death. When his body was dug up six months later it was still fresh and grasped a stick put in its hand. The body had to be dismembered and burned in order to stop the phantom from molesting people.

These vampire legends seem to stem from the Hebrew folklore about Lilith, the first wife of Adam, who was driven from Eden when she refused to be obedient to her husband. Lilith became an evil witch and a vampire, whose favorite pastime was sucking the blood from newborn babies. And her favorite disguise was that of a huge black cat, called El Broosha.

ESOTERIC CATS

If you look through most Tarot packs today you won't find any cats (except in the modern Tarot cards of the Cat People). But before the Marseilles pack was drawn (around 1800), the unnumbered Fool card was traditionally shown with a cat at his heels – in modern decks it is usually a dog. The cat symbolizes our lower nature trying to hold us back as we set out on the long road to enlightenment. This is a subconscious resistance, which is why the cat is biting the left leg rather than the right, since the left side of the body is the unconscious, intuitive side.

CATS AND ASTROLOGY

Surprisingly, there are no cats in Western or Eastern astrology, nor is there a constellation of the cat in astronomy. The French astronomer Joseph Lalande created a cat constellation, reputedly to spite Voltaire who disliked cats and mocked the fact that the cat had not managed to be included among the 33 animals that had constellations named after them. Lalande called his constellation Felis and included it in his map of the heavens because he was very fond of cats. He wrote, "I will let this figure scratch on the chart." It scratched for less than a hundred years, however, before being dropped on the grounds that it was "more than superfluous."

There is a legend that the cat was debarred from inclusion in the Chinese horoscope as punishment for its disgraceful behavior at Buddha's death. All the animals arrived to witness Buddha's entry to Nirvana except for the cat, which missed the event because it had stopped on the way to have a nap. In modern times the fourth Chinese zodiac sign is sometimes represented as a cat, but it was traditionally a hare.

THE FOOL

ALCHEMICAL CATS

In alchemy, the cat is seen as a counterpart to the lion. The lion, associated with the sun, is balanced by the cat's affinity with the moon. The lion symbolizes the male animus, the spirit; and the cat symbolizes the female anima, the soul. The cat and the lion represent the controlled and the untamed aspects of inner nature respectively. The cat also has another role in alchemy because its whiskers make the X-shape of the Greek letter *chi*, the initial letter of the Greek word for "chaos" (from which everything begins) and also of the Greek words for gold, crucible and time – the three unknown factors in the great work of alchemy. Perhaps that's why the letter X has come to represent the unknown factor to us?

THE CAT AND THE SERPENT

In addition to the legend that the cat failed to turn up to Buddha's funeral, there is another story that it did arrive but disgraced itself by being one of the only two animals that didn't weep. The other was the snake.

Cats and serpents are often linked together. As mentioned earlier, the Great Cat of Egyptian legend beheaded the serpent Apep every night so that Ra, the sun, could rise again the next morning. The Great Cat and Ra were dual aspects of the sleeping Ra, fighting the eternal battle of the sun cat against the serpent of darkness. In this myth, the cat also took the symbolic role of healer, since the serpent represented the forces of death, and illness.

In the early Gnostic work *Pistis Sophia*, Jesus tells Mary about a great serpent with its tail in its mouth that surrounds the world. The world has twelve punishment halls, each with one or more governors, several of whom have the face of a cat. Here the cat and the serpent are once again two parts of a single whole.

THE STORY OF THOR AND THE GRAY CAT
In Norse legends, the sky god Thor is challenged by a giant to perform various feats. One of these is to lift a giant gray cat from the floor, but Thor can only manage to raise one of its paws. The giant then tells Thor that the cat is really the serpent that encompasses Midgard (the earth) in disguise. So the cat and the serpent are one and the same, symbolizing the balance of the eternal forces of good and evil and the totality of everything on earth, both good and bad.

It seems that at the root of this symbolism is the image of the curled up cat, or the coiled snake, each with its tail in its mouth forming a circle. This circle represents eternity because it has no beginning or end, and totality because it encompasses everything. In alchemy, therefore, the cat represents chaos, while the snake symbolizes totality – everything that exists within the chaos, in terms of space and time.

CATS IN EGYPT

Many cultures worshiped lions – if you share your territory with them it's plain to see that they need to be treated with the utmost respect. The Babylonians, for example, saw the lion as a symbol of power and associated it with their great goddess of fertility and battle, Ishtar. So it must have been a heaven-sent gift to the Egyptians to find that they could tame the indigenous "miniature lions" – the wildcats of the region. The Egyptian veneration of cats seems to have been a lasting influence on virtually all European and Eastern attitudes to cats ever since.

THE CULT OF BASTET

Bastet was one of the minor Egyptian deities, originally an aspect of the moon goddess Isis. She became associated with cats early in their domestication and was quickly promoted to cult status as a major goddess. In some of the myths of Egypt, she is transformed into her lion-headed sister Sekhmet when she is angry and reverts to her gentler cat-self when calm – an obvious analogy for the wild lion and its tamed relative, the cat.

Bastet was also known as Bast, or Pasht, from which the word "puss" is thought to derive. Her cult was centered on the city of Bubastis in the Nile delta. The temple of Bubastis dates from about 2500 B.C., but in 945 B.C. the city was made the capital of Egypt, and Bastet was given precedence over all the other goddesses. Her temple was, by all accounts, an impressive sight. Herodotus visited it in about 450 B.C. and described it as being set on an island entirely surrounded by water except for the entrance passage. The Shrine, which was built of glittering red granite, was 500 feet long inside an inner and an outer enclosure. Bastet became the goddess of music, dance and revelry. She also had long-standing associations with fertility and the moon, which may well have led, in part, to the cat's later demonization by the Christians.

Bastet, who was portrayed either as a giant cat or as a woman with a cat's head, usually carried a sistrum. This was a kind of four-stringed rattle used by women to drive off evil spirits. A sistrum was also traditionally associated with fertility (and is probably the source of the old rhyme "hey diddle diddle, the cat and the fiddle"). The sistrum was also sacred to Isis, who herself occasionally took the form of a cat. Bastet often carried an aegis, or shield, which represented protection, and a basket – to put her kittens in.

THE CEREMONIES OF DEATH

Bubastis was the site of the most famous cat cemetery in Egypt. Literally hundreds of thousands of mummified cats have been found at Bubastis and other sites around Egypt (including the pyramids at Giza). Many of them had had their necks broken, suggesting that they had been the victims of sacrifice. Most of these sacrificed cats were very young when they were killed – rarely full-grown – so they may have been bred for this purpose. They were probably then sold as votive offerings.

Except in a sacrificial context, however, it was illegal to kill a cat in ancient Egypt, and the penalty for doing so was death. There is a story that in the 5th century B.C., the Persian king Cambyses managed to conquer Egypt by taking advantage of his enemies' strict observance of their own laws about cats. His soldiers all tied cats to the front of their shields, with the result that the Egyptians could not fight them for fear of injuring the cats and had to surrender.

When a cat died, all the members of its household went into mourning – a ritual that required them to shave off their eyebrows. This would have served as a sign to others that the family cat had died, but the eyebrows may also have symbolized the cat's fur. There has also been a suggestion that the crescent shape of the eyebrows recalled the moon and was therefore associated with the cat.

The cult of Bastet, and the regular festivals held at Bubastis in her honor, survived well into the Christian era. Every year, thousands of people would take the pilgrimage along the Nile to attend the annual festival. There would be great feasting and drinking, and sacrifices would be made – many of them probably mummified young cats. The festivals finally died out after nearly two thousand years, in 392 A.D., when the emperor Theodosius, who was a Christian, outlawed all pagan practices.

EASTERN CATS

The domestic cat was probably introduced to India and China from the West along the Silk Route – it had certainly arrived by 400 A.D. Buddhist monks may subsequently have introduced the cat to Japan from China sometime after the 6th century. It's likely that many of the legends and folktales about cats spread along with the animals themselves, which could account for the fact that many Eastern beliefs about cats are remarkably similar to Western folktales.

Cats are treated with great respect in most Eastern countries – in India it used to be a serious crime to kill a cat. Like the temple cats of Thailand and Burma, Japanese cats have also enjoyed legal protection in the past. The 10th-century emperor Ichijo once found a litter of kittens in a corner of his palace on a particularly propitious date and elevated cats to the status of nobility; they were treated royally and not allowed to work.

SAVIORS OF THE SILK INDUSTRY

Even when the silk industry was later threatened because mice were eating the silkworm cocoons, it was forbidden to use the protected cats to control the mice. The silk producers had to make do with statues of cats as "scarecats." Not surprisingly, this didn't impress the mice at all, and eventually the cats had to be put back to work to save the silk industry.

There is still a temple in Tokyo dedicated to cats – the temple of Gotokuji – which doubles as a place of worship and a cat necropolis. People hang prayer boards outside for sick or missing cats. The temple is protected by the spirit of Maneki-neko, a cat from Japanese folklore. She is always depicted with one front paw raised in greeting.

HARVEST CAT

The Chinese god of agriculture, Li-Shou, was worshiped in the form of a cat. After the harvest the people made sacrifices to him to protect the crops from vermin. It seems logical that a cat god would be the most appropriate to protect against rats and mice, and the traditional association between cats and fertility may also have played a part here – in this case to protect the fertility of the land.

Interestingly, this Chinese god parallels a minor European deity who was believed to protect crops and often took the form of a cat – known as the Corn Cat. Cats, of course, were linked with both the sun and the moon, and crops were traditionally planted according to the phases of the moon and then ripened by the sun.

CLASSICAL CATS

There are two theories about how domestic cats reached ancient Greece and the rest of Europe, but we're not sure which is correct. We know the Greeks kept cats as early as 550 B.C. because Aesop mentions them two or three times in his fables, which is the first time they're mentioned in Western literature. According to Aesop, the cat is a wily and deceptive animal, adept at tricking the other creatures, and even outwitting the fox.

One theory about the spread of domestic cats is that they followed the Romans in pursuit of the brown rat and the house mouse, which were slowly expanding their range across the classical world.

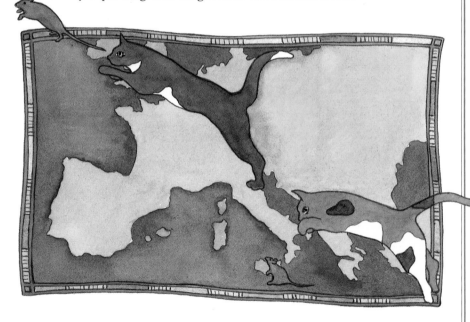

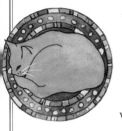

The other possibility is that the Greeks traded with the Egyptians for cats, which they seem to have wanted for pest control rather than as pets. That would explain why cats weren't common in Greece until about the same time that Christianity reached Egypt; before then the Egyptians would have considered cats too sacred to trade.

DIFFERENT ATTITUDES

The Romans didn't seem to realize how strongly the Egyptians felt about cats. There is a legend that the war between Rome and Egypt, which ended in the battle of Atrium and the deaths of Antony and Cleopatra, started because a Roman soldier in Egypt accidentally killed a cat.

The Greeks appear to have had a fairly practical approach to cats – they used them to control rats. Nevertheless, the Greeks clearly attributed some mystical powers to cats; Aristophanes wrote, "If a cat crosses the street it is a sign of bad luck."

The Romans, on the other hand, treated cats with far more respect. They seem to have been kept as house pets as well as ratters and mousers. One woman, whose body was found in Pompeii entombed in the lava from the eruption of Mount Vesuvius, had died still cradling her pet cat in her arms. We know that the Romans took cats as far as England with them. In Silchester, where there was a Roman brickworks, cat paw prints have been found on tiles. These were the first domestic cats in Britain.

This classical view probably did medieval cats little favor – centuries later, during the Middle Ages, the moon goddesses Diana/Artemis and Hecate came to be seen as the leaders of the witches. The cat, already deeply mistrusted, became tarred with the same brush.

FROM GODDESS TO WITCH

The Romans believed that the pupils of cats' eyes waxed and waned in accordance with the phases of the moon. They associated cats with the great moon goddess Diana, who was often depicted with a cat at her feet; the cat symbolized liberty. The cat's larger cousin, the lion, had many of the same associations in the classical world as it did in earlier Egyptian culture, and many of these applied to cats. For example, the Greeks linked lions with fertility and the underworld. They also connected them with water, and many of Greek fountains and springs were guarded by statues of lions. This probably accounts for the cat's supposed affinity with water (despite the fact that cats avoid water if they can). In many cultures cats were thought to be able to bring rain, or stop it.

In classical mythology, the gods all fled to Egypt from Mount Olympus to escape the monster Typhon. But they were afraid Typhon would follow them, so they all changed into different animals in order to hide from him. Diana – Artemis in Greek legend – transformed herself into a cat. There is a good reason for this choice of disguise. Artemis was essentially the Greek version of the Egyptian moon goddess, Bastet, who took the form of a cat; therefore, it's hardly surprising that Bastet's counterpart - Artemis/Diana – should follow her lead when in Egypt. Given the cat's intrinsic nature, it's also not surprising that it should have been associated with hunting – and Artemis and Diana were both goddesses of the hunt.

In the same flight from Olympus, Hecate also changed herself into a cat. Hecate was the Greek goddess of the underworld and the night, who represented Artemis' darker aspect. Hecate later became incorporated into Roman myth, as one of the three faces of the triple moon goddess: Luna (in the heavens), Diana (on earth) and Hecate (in the underworld). This triple goddess also took the form of a cat in order to mate with her brother, Lucifer. Their daughter, Aradia, was the teacher of witchcraft.

CATS IN NORTHERN EUROPE

In Norse mythology, cats were sacred to the fertility goddess Freyja, the patron of lovers and goddess of those slain in battle. Freyja was the Norse equivalent of Bastet and Hecate, with the same associations with fertility and death – not surprisingly she was also the Scandinavian moon goddess. Her chariot was originally drawn by lynxes (the domestic cat had not yet reached Northern Europe), but the lynxes were later portrayed as cats. Interestingly, Odin gave Freyja power over the "ninth world" – perhaps a reference to the ancient connection between cats and the number nine.

CAT GODDESSES OF PAGAN BRITAIN

The Celtic goddess Danu may have started out as a fertility goddess; little is known about her. However, she seems to have evolved into the terrifying "Black Annis" of the Dane hills in Leicestershire, England. Black Annis, who sometimes took the form of a cat, was said to have huge teeth and long nails and went out only at night, when she would kill and eat humans – preferably children – a tale remarkably reminiscent of the even more ancient Hebrew story of Lilith feeding on babies.

The Scottish Cailleach Bheur, or Blue Hag of Winter, also took the form of a cat. She was a goddess of winter, who was born each year on October 31 and brought the snow. She was eventually defeated by the goddess Brigit and turned to stone on April 30. This legend must owe a good deal to the story of Hecate, since it is so similar: in one version of the Greek legend, Persephone, daughter of the earth goddess Demeter, had to spend six months a year – each winter – in Hades, where she assumed the persona of Hecate.

THE DARK AGES

The association between cats and fertility was widespread in the Dark Ages; throughout Northern Europe and beyond, cats were sacrificed and buried beneath fruit trees and in fields to bring luck to the harvest. It's likely that the Corn Cat, which reputedly protected the growing crops was an adaptation of Freyja. The Corn Cat supposedly hid in a special sheaf of grain, or "corn," after the harvest and waited for the spring sowing when it would emerge to watch over the next crop. The Corn Cat myth is probably the origin of the widespread practice of ritually killing a cat as the last sheaf of grain is cut. This practice persists in a symbolic form in many parts of Europe where people dress as cats, or even decorate a real cat with ribbons, to celebrate the end of the harvest.

CATS AND WITCHCRAFT

In the 13th century, people were becoming disillusioned with the Church and the whole structure of society. The Church needed a scapegoat, and it picked on witchcraft – after all, old women were less likely than anyone to put up a serious defense. Over the next few centuries, thousands of women throughout Europe were executed for witchcraft, and many cats were condemned along with them.

There are several reasons why the Church treated cats so appallingly during the medieval witch hunts. For one thing, cats had long been associated with women, by the Egyptians, Greeks and Romans in particular. These mythologies had also linked cats with the underworld as well as the moon with all its unconscious and darker mysteries.

In its attempts to Christianize Europe, the Church tried to discredit the pagan gods and goddesses that it was trying to depose. It condemned the major goddesses of the underworld as witches – goddesses such as Diana, Artemis, Hecate and Freyja, who of course were all associated with cats, having been descended from Bastet.

The Church had another great argument for condemning cats – they were mentioned only once in the Bible, and then only in the Apocrypha, where it simply says that bats and birds shall sit on the bodies of idols, and cats also. This omission, at least as far as the Old Testament is concerned, is probably due to the fact that the Jews disliked anything that had been sacred to the Egyptians who had ruled them for so long. So in condemning cats, the Church could not be accused of contradicting the word of God.

The combination of all these factors meant that for over five centuries the cat suffered the most dreadful tortures throughout Christendom.

THE MEDIEVAL WITCH

In 1565, Agnes Waterhouse, her daughter Joan and a woman named Elizabeth Francis were tried for witchcraft in England. Elizabeth apparently had a white spotted cat called Sathan that she fed on bread, milk and her own blood. This cat was supposedly responsible for, among other things, killing a man who had made Elizabeth pregnant and then refused to marry her. The cat also instructed her in how to abort the unwanted pregnancy. Elizabeth then gave the cat to Agnes, who turned it into a toad. It then wreaked havoc in the neighborhood, allegedly killing numerous livestock. Elizabeth and Agnes were both hanged for witchcraft.

The most enduring image of the witch's familiar is a black cat – in fact, as late as the 19th century a woman in southeast England was thrown into a pit simply for the sin of having a black cat. As well as flying on broomsticks, sometimes in the shape of cats, witches were also thought to ride through the sky on cats. It was commonly thought that a witch could turn herself into a cat. According to some, she could do this nine times during her life; this was sometimes thought to be the origin of the belief that cats have nine lives. However, both these beliefs date back to a far earlier association between cats and the number nine.

There is still a saying in some parts that you should "never speak ill of anyone in front of a cat." The logic behind this was that the cat might not have been a cat at all, but a witch in disguise. In Hungary, they believed that most cats became witches somewhere between the ages of seven and twelve, so they incised the animal's skin with a cut in the shape of a cross in order to prevent the transformation.

According to an 18th-century account from the north of England, one night "Robert Tinbull was spelled on the bridge over an hour by Hester Dale, the old witch of Marrick. His horse would not move until Tom Wilson came along with a rowan staff. Then they both saw Hester run over the road as a black cat. They both knew it was her, because she had meant him harm for a good while."

CATS AND THE DEVIL

According to medieval folklore, cats were actually invented by the Devil. And cats, particularly black ones, were often believed to be the Devil in disguise. People certainly thought so in Ireland – it was a traditional greeting, on entering a house, to say "God save all here, except the cat." In Slavonia, many of the peasants were convinced that the Devil lived in the body of a black cat. They would avoid these cats at night because they believed that during the hours of darkness the Devil had the power to turn back suddenly into human form and attack them.

In the 17th century, a woman in Denmark was prosecuted for having a child that had the head of a cat – which supposedly proved that she had been consorting with the Devil, and this half-kitten was his offspring. In fact, as in other cases from that period, the baby was presumably suffering from some deformity such as anencephaly.

Cats were a common ingredient in ceremonies to raise the Devil. In the Scottish Highlands there was a rite that called for four or more people to throw a live cat backward into a kiln that had two doors. According to a 17th-century description of the rite, one person would then climb underneath a cauldron, one would chant the invocation, and another would stand facing the Devil when he appeared. The people then threw the cat in his face, after which the Devil had to answer their questions and grant their requests.

THE TEMPLARS
AND THE CATHARS

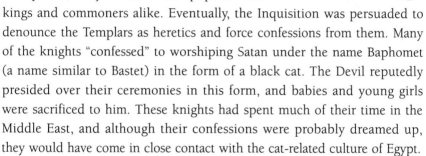

The Knights Templar, an order of knights created in the 12th century to provide safe passage to pilgrims visiting the Holy Land, were lauded and praised when they were first formed. However, as they gained more wealth and power, they became less popular with kings and commoners alike. Eventually, the Inquisition was persuaded to denounce the Templars as heretics and force confessions from them. Many of the knights "confessed" to worshiping Satan under the name Baphomet (a name similar to Bastet) in the form of a black cat. The Devil reputedly presided over their ceremonies in this form, and babies and young girls were sacrificed to him. These knights had spent much of their time in the Middle East, and although their confessions were probably dreamed up, they would have come in close contact with the cat-related culture of Egypt.

Several religious groups of the time were similarly accused, including the Albigensians and Waldensians. Another medieval sect accused of heresy were the Cathars. One 12th-century historian, Alain de Lille, claimed that the Cathars were named after cats because that was the form in which the Devil appeared to them. This was completely untrue (their own name for themselves was Bon Hommes), but it clearly shows the prevailing attitude to cats – an attitude that would color the official view of cats for many centuries.

CATS AND CHRISTIANITY

According to one Christian folk story, when Jesus was born a cat gave birth to a litter of kittens in the stable at the same time. The Madonna asked all the animals in the stable to help Jesus to sleep, but none of them could until a small gray tabby kitten snuggled up next to him in the manger. Jesus fell asleep to the sound of her purring, and the Madonna rewarded the cat by allowing all tabbies to wear a letter M on their foreheads from then on.

Early Christianity doesn't seem to have felt threatened by cats. They were probably introduced to Ireland in the 4th or 5th century by the monks, who included illustrations of them in many of their manuscripts. The 8th-century Book of Kells, for example, contains many beautiful pictures of cats. They seem to symbolize judgment, often presiding over mice or rats, which represent human souls.

The first Christians accepted cats and absorbed pagan cat beliefs into their religion. St. Agatha supposedly turned into an angry cat (reminiscent of Sekhmet) to berate women who worked on her feast day. She was even known as Santo Gato, or St. Cat. And the cat and mouse were both sacred to St. Gertrude. Given this practice of assimilating pagan and Christian beliefs, it's likely that associations between cats and the Madonna developed in a similar way, based on the strong links between cats and earlier mother goddesses. The Christian festival of the Assumption on August 15, which celebrates the taking up of the body and soul of the Virgin Mary into heaven, was superimposed on the pagan feast day of Diana/Artemis.

The Madonna and child were often painted with a cat, the ancient fertility symbol, by Leonardo da Vinci and other artists. It seems that

Christianity had, perhaps unwittingly, absorbed Bastet's cats into their own beliefs, partly via the Greeks and Romans. This Christian cat was the "good cat" created by God, according to Christian folklore, to combat the mouse created by the Devil.

BAD CATS

The cat, by association with witches, became an ideal scapegoat for the Church when it tightened its stranglehold on paganism. The medieval Church believed that groups of women worshiped the Roman goddess Diana, having been ensnared into her service by Satan. One 12th-century Bishop of 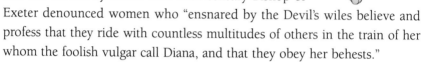 Exeter denounced women who "ensnared by the Devil's wiles believe and profess that they ride with countless multitudes of others in the train of her whom the foolish vulgar call Diana, and that they obey her behests."

The cult of Diana (which some historians believe existed only in the imagination of the Church) was the first victim of the Church's persecution of "witches." And the cat that had traditionally sat at Diana's feet became her familiar when the Church began to view her as a witch.

Although the cat had once represented the divine fertility of the Madonna in art, it now came to represent stealth and treachery, and as such was associated with Judas. Many paintings of the last supper include a cat sitting at the feet of Judas – known as a "Judas cat." Once the heretical Manicheans, Waldensians, Albigensians, Cathars and Templars had all "confessed" to worshiping Satan in the form of a black cat, there was no stopping the outburst of hatred toward cats. From the late Middle Ages onward, Christians began to persecute cats mercilessly.

During the Renaissance, the inappropriately named Pope Innocent VIII ordered that every cat in Christendom should be killed. Millions of cats were destroyed – most were burned – until Louis XIII stopped the practice in the early 17th century. Interestingly, this may well have made the impact of the Black Death considerably worse, since there were not enough cats to kill the rats that carried the disease.

Eventually, medieval superstition and belief in witches began to wane, and as European societies became more health conscious in the 18th and 19th centuries, when many fatal diseases were rife and science had not yet fully explained their causes, the cat was at least partially forgiven by the Christian Church. When Napoleon's army was in Egypt there was an outbreak of plague. Cats were brought into the army camps to control the rats, and the threat of widespread plague was removed. The cat's value in keeping down vermin, coupled with its exemplary washing habits, led to its symbolic association with hygiene and cleanliness – which was, of course, considered next to godliness.

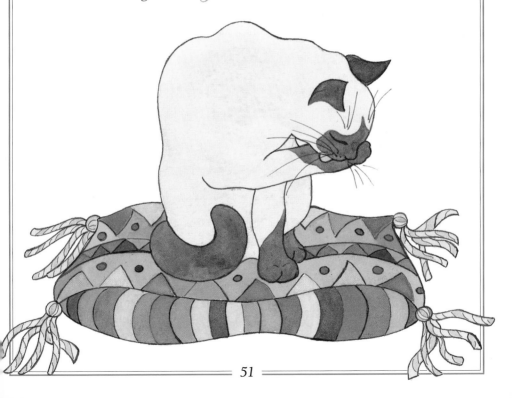

THE BLACK CAT

The black cat seems to have been a genetic mutation that originated in Phoenicia, perhaps around 1000 B.C. The Egyptians regarded black cats as being particularly lucky, but since the Middle Ages they have traditionally been associated with the Devil. The Norse goddess Freyja was originally portrayed riding in a chariot pulled by cats; the Christians turned Freyja into a witch and her cats became black horses. After seven years' work, however, the horses were rewarded by being turned into witches – disguised as black cats.

Black cats have also traditionally been seen as cures for numerous complaints including shingles, whooping cough and, especially, sties. In the case of sties this is presumably a form of sympathetic magic associating cats with sight because of their ability to see in the dark. Unfortunately for the cats, the vast majority of the recorded cures involve killing a black cat and then drinking its blood, roasting and eating its heart, burning its head to ashes and other similar practices. At the very least it was almost always necessary to cut off its tail.

Black cats are considered lucky in some places – although they are usually still treated warily. There is a belief that touching a black cat is lucky; in some places it will even grant you a wish. Bastet was a goddess of healing, among other things, and this may account for the cat's supposed power to bestow good or ill on people. Cats, and especially black ones, were linked with witches and, therefore, with the ability to control storms and winds at sea. Sailors' wives used to keep black cats to protect their husbands at sea – in some fishing villages black cats became so valuable that they were almost impossible to keep because they were often stolen. 𝕁

CATS AND THE SUPERNATURAL

There is a good deal of evidence that cats are far more sensitive than we are to unexplained psychic phenomena – or ghosts. There have been many well-documented cases of cats "seeing" ghosts that their human companions could not. One such case concerns a woman whose cat had died. A friend came to visit one day, bringing her own Siamese cat. This cat wandered over to the cushion where the dead cat had always slept, and suddenly it started to arch its back and spit, exactly as though it were facing another cat. A little later, the owner of the house opened the French windows, at about the time her old cat had been in the habit of going out through them. Almost instantly the Siamese cat stood up, crossed over to the cushion and curled up on it – as if it had just been vacated by the other cat.

THE GIFT OF SECOND SIGHT

This strange sensitivity in cats must have been recognized for thousands of years. Bede, the historian and monk, wrote in the 8th century of ritual cat sacrifice in Scotland in which the tortured cats helped raise the Black Cat Spirits, which gave the gift of second sight. The Hebrew Talmud has instructions for seeing into the spirit world that involve burning a black cat to powder and putting the powder in one's eyes.

In areas of the Gold Coast, shamen wear catskins round their necks to help them speak to the spirits. The Egyptians also seem to have credited cats with the ability to see spirits. Similarly, the ancient Britons believed that staring deep into the eyes of a cat allowed you to see into the spirit world. (This belief probably referred to the native wildcat of Britain.) Presumably people observed cats apparently "seeing" spirits – the Egyptians of course would have fitted this into their view of cats quite naturally, since cats were also strongly associated with the underworld.

THE CAT AS GHOST

Sometimes it is the cat that appears in spectral form. In 1968, the artist Tom McAssey was painting in the gallery at the Dower House at Killakee in Ireland. The house is supposed to have a number of ghosts including a demonic black cat that has been seen intermittently since the 18th century. The door to the gallery, which was locked, suddenly swung open. Seeing a shadowy figure in the hall, McAssey concluded that someone was playing a game with him. So he called, "Come in, I can see you." A voice answered simply, "You can't see me." McAssey shut the door firmly and returned along the gallery. Half way back he looked over his shoulder – to see a huge black cat staring at him through red eyes. 🖌

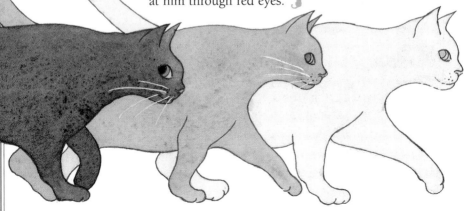

CAT SUPERSTITIONS

In the early 17th century, Edward Topsell wrote that "the breath and savor of cats consume the radical humor and destroy the lungs.". Some people, of course, are allergic to cats, but when the witch hunts were rife it was often thought that cats deliberately infected people.

It was quite common to cure illnesses by transferring them to a cat. In one account from 1750, a woman with a swollen hand held her finger in a cat's ear. Within two hours, the pain had gone – but the cat was in such agony that it took two men to hold it.

MAY CATS AND BLACKBERRY KITTENS

The Christians pronounced the month of May an evil month, because it was the month of the old pagan festival of Beltane. Consequently, kittens born in May were thought to be bad, and many people believed they should be killed. Beltane was the ancient fertility festival, which perhaps strengthened its association with cats. It was thought that May kittens would bring snakes into the house, and there's an old saying "May chets bad luck begets and sure to make dirty cats." In some places, kittens born just after Michaelmas (September 29) were known as blackberry kittens and were thought to be especially wild.

LUCKY OR NOT?

Is a black cat crossing your path good luck or bad luck? It depends where you are. In Japan or England, for example, it's good luck. Although in some parts of Britain it's considered unlucky unless you spit. When the early English settlers first came to North America, they brought with them the prevailing view that a black cat crossing your path was bad luck. Their negative view has been more persistent than that of their counterparts who remained in England.

It is considered unlucky for a woman to have a black cat cross her path on her way to her wedding (harking back to ancient associations with fertility). In modern times there is a belief that if a black cat crosses from left to right in front of your car you will get a puncture. One of the fairer superstitions on the subject is that if the cat is walking toward you it will bring you luck, and if it has its back to you it is unlucky.

And in one somewhat self-fulfilling version, if a black cat crosses your path and does you no evil, it's lucky.

THE CAT AS ILL OMEN

In parts of France, it was bad luck for a whole year if you saw a cat on January 1. In other places, the sight of cats playing in the morning guaranteed that the whole day would be wasted. You weren't safe at night either, since to meet a cat at midnight was to meet Satan himself. It might have been safer just to keep your eyes permanently closed – were it not for the fact that it was also a bad sign to dream about a cat.

THE SHIP'S CAT

Cats have a long association with sailors, perhaps because the weather is of particular importance to them. Japanese sailors always took a cat to sea with them to warn them if bad weather was coming. In much of Europe and the West, as well, cats were often taken to sea because they were thought to predict or even control the weather. It was believed, for example, that if the cat mewed you had a difficult journey ahead of you, and if you threw a cat overboard you would raise a storm.

Sailors and their wives often thought that if you "shut up" a cat in a cupboard or under a tub, it would raise the wind. If the boat was trapped in harbor the sailors would often say that someone on shore had shut up the cat, and sailors' wives would shut the cat up to keep their husbands at home.

The word "cat" used to be taboo among the fishermen of Shetland, especially when they were setting their lines.

A black cat running ahead of you on your way to the fishing boat is a good sign, but if it crosses your path you should go home and forget the idea of fishing for the day. If the day's haul is poor, there is a Scottish expression "We've met the cat i' the mornin'." This has come to describe any failed venture.

WHY DO CATS HAVE NINE LIVES?

The idea that cats have nine lives seems to date back to ancient Egypt, like so many other beliefs about cats. Nine is a sacred number, being three times three – many cultures worshiped trinities so the number three was always important. The nine gods of ancient Heliopolis were all linked with the cat, and the Egyptians, who were very concerned with numerology, probably linked the cat with the number nine. This connection has since been adapted into all sorts of beliefs, such as cats having nine lives, or witches being able to transform themselves into cats nine times in their lives.

THE CAT'S SIXTH SENSE

The Egyptian word for a cat was *mau*, which means "to see" or "the seer." This may have derived from the cat's association with the eye of Horus. Or it may simply have been the sound a cat makes. On the other hand, it may also have had something to do with the cat's apparent ability to foresee future events. Some of the skills associated with this "sixth sense" can be scientifically explained nowadays. Others, frankly, are still baffling – at least for the time being.

A SENSE OF DANGER
Cats are incredibly sensitive to vibrations, and this seems to be the explanation for their strange ability to anticipate disasters such as earthquakes, volcanoes and wartime air raids. Many people who live on the slopes of active volcanoes keep cats to warn them of eruptions – and with good reason.

One example of this is the story of a cat called Toto, who lived with his owners near Mount Vesuvius. One night in 1944, Toto woke his owner by repeatedly scratching him on the cheek. Despite the owner's angry resistance, Toto wouldn't stop. The man's wife finally decided that the cat's behavior was a sign that the volcano was about to erupt and insisted they throw a few things together and leave the town. An hour later Vesuvius erupted, killing over thirty people and burying their house in molten lava.

PSI-TRAILING
Cats' ability to find their way home over implausibly long distances is legendary – the world record is held by a cat that traveled 1,500 miles back

to its home. An ancient Hebrew folktale provides an interesting clue as to how long this extraordinary feline ability has been observed. The legend claims that when Adam and Eve and the animals were expelled from the garden of Eden, the cat was the only one that memorized the route, and it still knows the way back to the gates of heaven.

PERFECT TIMING

Many cats have an unerring ability to judge the time, and perhaps this helped cement their association with the sun and the moon, which always know exactly when to rise and set.

The French writer Alexandre Dumas had a cat, Mysouff, with a most remarkable talent. When Dumas returned from work in the evening, the cat always met him in the same place at the end of the street, arriving there at the same moment as Dumas. However, occasionally Dumas would be delayed. On these occasions Dumas' mother would open the door at her usual time, and Mysouff, instead of jumping from his cushion, would refuse to move. Eventually, the cat would get up, leave the house, and arrive at the corner of the street at the same moment as Dumas.

CATS AND DEATH

Cats are associated with death because they represent Hecate, herself the goddess of death and the underworld, and they are often seen as omens of death. In Germany there was a belief that if a sick person saw two cats fighting it was a sign of that person's approaching death. This seems to derive from the view that the two cats – one good and one evil – were in fact the Devil and an angel arguing over the soul of the dying person. It was often believed that if a cat left the house of a sick person, he or she would die soon. If the cat itself was dying, it was often thrown out of the house for fear that once it died, death might wait for someone else.

There are several strange and well-documented stories of cats appearing to people shortly before the death of someone close to them. In one example, from the 1890s, a young woman, seeing a strange cat in the corridor as she came downstairs from her sick grandfather's room, followed it into a room from which there was no exit, only to find that the cat had disappeared. The next day her grandfather died. The young woman told her mother, who had a similar story. The day before her husband had died, which was some years before, she had seen a cat walk around his bed – when she went to follow it, it had disappeared, despite there being no way out of the room without passing her.

THE LUNAR SPHERE
There is another reason why cats are traditionally associated with death, which is particularly apparent in medieval occult texts. The earth was seen to be at the center of the heavens, surrounded by a series of concentric spheres, one outside the other – the spheres of the planets. It was

necessary, at birth and death, to pass through the sphere of the moon (which was thought to be crystalline rather than gaseous) in order to reach the spheres of the other planets beyond and, eventually, arrive in heaven.

It was often thought that the sphere of the moon was the place of purgatory, where any impurity in the soul had to be purged before it was possible to pass on to heaven. Babies on their way to be born could pass through freely, but the souls of the dead had to face the demons of purgatory before they could pass through. This mystic link between cats, the moon and the demons may have fueled later associations of cats with witchcraft and evil – it is certainly one of the most enduring symbolisms and still colors our view of cats today.

For Frey, Hecate, Ishtar, Ra,

Ttattoo – and Pan